D1399025

HURT

First published 1990
by Cherrytree Press Ltd
Windsor Bridge Road
Bath, Avon BA2 3AX England

Copyright © Cherrytree Press Ltd 1990

First published in the United States 1991
by Raintree Publishers

Copyright © 1991 Raintree Publishers Limited Partnership

Library of Congress Number: 90-46540

1 2 3 4 5 6 7 8 9   95 94 93 92 91

Library of Congress Cataloging-in-Publication Data

Amos, Janine.
   Feelings/by Janine Amos; illustrated by Gwen Green.
   Cover title.
   Contents: [1] Afraid—[2] Angry—[3] Hurt—[4] Jealous—
[5] Lonely—[6] Sad.
   1. Emotions—Case studies—Juvenile literature. [1. Emotions.]
I. Green, Gwen, ill.   II. Title.
BF561.A515   1991
152.4—dc20   90-46540
                                         CIP
                                         AC

   ISBN 0-8172-3775-5 (v. 1); ISBN 0-8172-3776-3 (v. 2); ISBN
0-8172-3777-1 (v. 3); ISBN 0-8172-3778-X (v. 4); ISBN 0-8172-
3779-8 (v. 5); ISBN 0-8172-3780-1 (v. 6).

HURT

By Janine Amos
Illustrated by Gwen Green

RAINTREE PUBLISHERS
Milwaukee

BILLY'S STORY

The bell rang. Time to go home! All the kids dashed out of their classrooms onto the playground.

"There he goes! Tiny little Billy!" shouted some boys from Billy's room. Billy kept his head down. He pretended that he didn't hear.

"Hey, runt!" called another boy. "What's it like down there, shorty?" The other kids laughed.

As usual, Billy felt his eyes fill with tears. His face turned red. As the teasing went on, he felt worse and worse. Then he turned and shouted at the boys.

"Leave me alone! I hate you!" Billy started to run. He wished he wasn't the smallest boy in the class.

At home, Billy tore open the front door and slammed it behind him. He didn't want to see anyone, so he raced for his room.

"Hey, Billy!" called his dad. "Come here a minute."

Billy went into the kitchen. He pulled off his backpack and sent it skidding across the floor.

Why didn't Billy want to see anyone when he got home?

"I hate being little," Billy said angrily. He told his dad how the other boys always teased him.

"I know just how you feel," said his dad when Billy had finished. "I was always the shortest boy in school."

Billy was surprised. He'd never thought of his dad as being small before.

Then his mom came into the kitchen. She went over to Billy's dad and kissed him. Then she gave Billy a hug.

"I like you both however you are," she said. She smiled. "So, Billy, what do those boys call you? Let me guess. Shorty?"

"Yeah," said Billy.

"Runt?" guessed his dad.

"That's right," said Billy.

"Shrimp?" asked his mom, giggling.

"Yes," answered Billy, "and pipsqueak!"

"Pipsqueak?" laughed his mom and dad together. "That must be the silliest one!"

The next morning, the boys were waiting outside the school when Billy got there.

"Here comes the little squirt!" they called. But this time Billy didn't feel like crying, and he didn't run away. Instead, he remembered laughing with his mom and dad.

"Squirt! Ha!" he thought. "That's not half as funny as pipsqueak!"

How did Billy's mother and father help? Who could help you if you were feeling hurt?

Feeling like Billy

Have you ever been teased, like Billy? If you have, you know how much it hurts. Most people get teased at some time or another. It's especially hard when you are teased about something you can't change, as Billy was.

Don't help teasers

Some mean people like to make fun of others. They think it's funny to see someone get upset. If you're being teased, try not to show what you're feeling. Then the teasers might give up. Don't let teasers know that you care.

Talking about it

If you're feeling like Billy, tell someone. Talk to someone you trust. Like Billy and his parents, you could talk about the silly things that teasers say. Together, you might think up some answers to give the next time someone teases you. You could think of things to say that show you don't care.

Think about it

Read the stories in this book. Think about the people in the stories. Do you ever feel the way they do? Next time you feel hurt, ask yourself some questions: What can I do to help myself? Who can I talk to? Then find someone you trust, like a teacher, a parent, or a friend. Tell that person how you're feeling, just as Billy did.

ANNIE'S STORY

Annie sat in front of the TV. She wasn't really watching the show, but it was something to do.

"Annie," called her mother from the kitchen. "Come and tell me what happened in school today." Her mother was getting supper ready, and Annie knew that she should be helping. But Annie didn't want to talk. Nothing was the same since her father had left home.

Annie heard her brother Matthew coming in. She liked Matthew, but he was getting on her nerves lately. He was always trying to make her laugh—or talk about Dad.

"Hey, kiddo!" said Matthew, sitting down next to Annie. "What's going on?"

"Oh, be quiet!" snapped Annie. She didn't want to talk to Matthew.

Why do you think Annie doesn't want to talk to anyone?

At supper, Annie was very quiet. She knew that her father was coming later. Every Friday evening he came to get Annie and her brother for the weekend. They stayed with him in his new apartment, and he took them somewhere special as a treat.

"Did you pack yet, Annie?" her mother asked.
"I'm not going," said Annie.
"You've always gone before," said her mother.
"Well, I'm not going this time," replied Annie.
But her mother sent her upstairs to pack anyway.

"You'll be okay once you get there," said Matthew. "We always have fun with Dad."

"Oh, you don't know anything!" shouted Annie.

Matthew turned red and shouted back at her, "He's my dad too, you know!"

Why doesn't Annie want to go to her father's? How do you think she feels?

When their father arrived, he gave Annie and Matthew each a big hug. Annie tried not to hug back.

"What shall we do this weekend, Annie?" he asked. "It's your turn to choose."

"I don't care," said Annie.

The next day they drove out to the country. When they had parked, Matthew and their father went to the back of the car. Annie followed slowly. Their dad took two huge kites out of the trunk. Matthew's kite was red with a dragon painted on it. Annie's had different colors and a long tail. Matthew was excited.

"Thanks, Dad!" he said. "Can we fly them now?"

"Sure," said his father. "The wind's just right. I'll help you get them going."

Annie followed behind, dragging her kite along the ground.

Soon Matthew had learned how to let the wind lift his kite high into the sky.

"Shall we get yours going, Annie?" her father asked.

"No, thanks," said Annie.

"Okay, but pick it up or it will rip," he warned.

"Good," said Annie quietly.

At the top of a hill Annie sat down. She could see Matthew in the distance, flying his red kite.

"Don't you like your kite?" asked her father. He sat down next to her. Annie was feeling mad and sad at the same time, but mostly she felt like crying.

"You're mad at me, aren't you?" asked her father.

How do you think Annie's father is feeling?

He went on talking. "I know I hurt you by leaving home, Annie. I'm really sorry. I miss being with you and Matthew every day."

"You'll never come back home to live with us, will you?" asked Annie.

"No," said her father. "But we'll see each other every week. I'll make sure of that."

"It hurts," said Annie. "I feel awful."

"I know," said her father. "Your mother and I hurt each other, and now we're hurting you."

"It does feel better to talk about it, though," said Annie.

When Annie got into bed that night, she gave her dad a big kiss.

"I didn't thank you for my kite," she said.

"Then you did like it after all?" her father asked.

"Yeah, it's neat," said Annie, "but talking is better."

How do you think Annie feels now?

Feeling like Annie

Have you been hurt, like Annie? If someone you love goes away, it hurts very much. You know that it's not your fault, but that doesn't change things. Sometimes it's hard to understand adults and the things they do.

It helps to talk

Talking can help you feel better. Talking isn't easy when you're very upset, and there's so much you want to say. But, as Annie found out, it is a good idea to share your feelings. Try talking to someone you trust. It helps.

JERRY'S STORY

Jerry was eating breakfast with his family. It seemed to be taking a long time this morning, and Jerry was in a hurry. He was going skateboarding with his friend Mark. Jerry was a whole year younger than Mark, but he was almost as good on his skateboard. Jerry gobbled down the last of his cornflakes. Then he swallowed the last big mouthful of orange juice.

"Hey!" said Jerry's dad. "What's the big hurry? Where's the fire?"

"I'm meeting Mark down at the corner at nine o'clock," said Jerry. "I don't want to be late."

When Jerry got to the corner of the block, he was five minutes early. He sat down to wait for Mark. He watched a lady feeding some pigeons. He practiced balancing on his skateboard. He counted the cars at the traffic light. Six of them were red. He watched the ants running along the sidewalk.

Jerry waited a long time. But Mark didn't show up.

What would you do if you were Jerry?

Finally, Jerry walked over to Mark's house. Maybe everyone was still in bed. Jerry rang the doorbell.

"Hi, Jerry," said Mark's mother. "Mark's not here. He already went to the park to skateboard."

"Oh," said Jerry.

Jerry walked to the park. He felt very lonely and upset. He was sure he'd been at the corner on time. Why had Mark gone without him? What had Jerry done wrong? Jerry didn't understand.

At the park, Jerry saw Mark with some other boys on the skateboard track. Slowly Jerry went over to them.

"I've been waiting for you at the corner," said Jerry. "Did you forget?"

"No," said Mark, standing on his skateboard. "I knew you'd turn up here sooner or later. Hey, watch this one!"

How would you feel now if you were Jerry?

Jerry watched Mark for a while. Then he skated a little bit. But he didn't really feel like playing now.

"I'm going over to my grandfather's," he called. "Bye!" But no one heard him.

Jerry's grandfather lived just a block away from the park. He was always happy to see Jerry. Soon Jerry was eating brownies and drinking milk. Jerry told his grandfather about Mark.

"So now you're feeling hurt?" asked his grandfather when Jerry had finished. Jerry nodded.

"I guess Mark should have waited for you," his grandfather said.

"He promised he would!" said Jerry.

"Well," said his grandfather, "what do you want to bet that Mark didn't mean to be unkind?"

"Maybe he thinks I'm too young to play with him," said Jerry.

"No," said his grandfather, "I don't think so. I think Mark was just in too much of a hurry to have fun. Now, *you* get back to that park, and *you* have some fun!"

Jerry felt better after talking to his grandfather. He went back to the park and watched for a while. Mark and the others were still there. Then Mark saw him.

"Hey, Jerry, come on!" Mark shouted. "Show these guys how you do that trick!"

Jerry ran to join his friend. "Grandpa was right again," he thought, smiling.

How did Jerry's grandfather help? Who can you talk to when you feel hurt?

Feeling like Jerry

Sometimes people hurt us without meaning to. Mark didn't keep his promise to Jerry. That wasn't very nice of him. But Mark didn't mean to hurt Jerry. If you're feeling hurt, ask yourself a question: Did that person mean to upset me? You might find that no one meant to be unkind, and that helps.

Feeling bad

Sometimes being hurt makes us feel bad about ourselves. When someone hurts us, we may think we deserved it somehow. Try not to think like that. No one deserves to be hurt.

Feeling good

When you're upset, it helps to be with someone you know well. That's why Jerry went to see his grandfather. If you feel bad, spend some time with a friend until you're feeling good again.

Feeling hurt

Think about the stories in this book. Billy, Annie, and Jerry were each hurt in different ways, and they each found someone to help. If you're hurt, talking about it will help you too.

If you are feeling frightened or unhappy, don't keep it to yourself. Talk to an adult you can trust:

- one of your parents or other relatives
- a friend's parent or other relative
- a teacher
- the principal
- someone else at school
- a neighbor
- someone at a church, temple, or synagogue

You can also find someone to talk to about a problem by calling places called "hotlines." One hotline is **Child Help,** which you can call from anywhere in the United States. Just call

1-800-422-4453

from any telephone. You don't need money to call.

Or look in the phone book to find another phone number of people who can help. Try

- Children and Family Service
- Family Service

Remember you can always call the Operator in any emergency. Just dial 0 or press the button that says 0 on the telephone.